COMING IN TO LAND

COMING IN TO LAND

Selected Poems 1975–2015

ANDREW MOTION

ecco

An Imprint of HarperCollinsPublishers

HarperCollins

PUBLISHERS

Since 1817

COMING IN TO LAND. Copyright © 2017 by Andrew Motion. All rights reserved.
Printed in the United States of America. No part of this book may be used or
reproduced in any manner whatsoever without written permission except in the
case of brief quotations embodied in critical articles and reviews. For information,
address HarperCollins Publishers, 195 Broadway, New York, NY 10007.

HarperCollins books may be purchased for educational, business, or sales
promotional use. For information, please email the Special Markets Department
at SPsales@harpercollins.com.

FIRST EDITION

Designed by Jane Treuhaft

Library of Congress Cataloging-in-Publication Data has been applied for.

ISBN 978-0-06-264407-7

17 18 19 20 21   RRD   10 9 8 7 6 5 4 3 2 1

For Alan Hollinghurst

Contents

III.

POEMS *(2009–2015)*

I.

POEMS

(1975–2008)

ANNE FRANK HUIS

Even now, after twice her lifetime of grief
and anger in the very place, whoever comes
to climb these narrow stairs, discovers how
the bookcase slides aside, then walks through
shadow into sunlit rooms, can never help

but break her secrecy again. Just listening
is a kind of guilt: the Westerkirk repeats
itself outside, as if all time worked round
towards her fear, and made each stroke
die down on guarded streets. Imagine it—

four years of whispering, and loneliness,
and plotting, day by day, the Allied line
in Europe with a yellow chalk. What hope
she had for ordinary love and interest
survives her here, displayed above the bed

as pictures of her family; some actors;
fashions chosen by Princess Elizabeth.
And those who stoop to see them find
not only patience missing its reward,
but one enduring wish for chances

like my own: to leave as simply
as I do, and walk at ease
up dusty tree-lined avenues, or watch
a silent barge come clear of bridges
settling their reflections in the blue canal.

SERENADE

There were the two ponies
and there was Serenade,
which belonged to my mother.

Though 'who belonged' would be better,
in view of the girlish head-lift she had,
and her flounce to and fro in the lumpy field,
and that big womanish rump I always gave a wide berth to.

When the blacksmith came to shoe her,
which was seldom in summer
but otherwise often,
she would let him hoist and stretch out first one hind leg,
then the other
with a definitely melancholy, embarrassed restraint.

The blacksmith was ferret-faced and rat-bodied,
hardly man enough to keep aloft the great weight
of one-foot-at-a-time,
although he did keep it sort of aloft,
crouched over double and bent at the knees,
to make a peculiar angle which held each hoof still
on his battle-scarred apron.

He would set up shop
under the covered entrance-way
between our house and the stable block:
a ramshackle clapboard affair,

black (or black weathering to green),
with swallows' mud villages proliferating in the rafters.

I liked it there in the drive-through,
which was also where we parked the car
(but not on his days)—
for the oil maps on the dusty cement
brilliant as the wet skin of a trout,
and for the puzzling swallow-shit patterns,
and most of all for that place by the corner drain
where a grass-snake had appeared once,
an electric-green, sleepy-looking marvel
which, when it disappeared, left a print of itself
that stayed in the mind for ever.

The blacksmith always did cold shoeing,
prising off each thin moon-crescent,
then carving the hoof with a bone-handled,
long-bladed knife.

The miracle of no pain!

Serenade gone loose in her skin,
her strength out of her,
so she seemed suspended in water,
her hypnotised breathing steady,
the smell of piss
and musty hay
and ammonia sweat coming off her,
her head dropping down,
eyes half closed now,

and me a boy
watching the earth-stained sole of her hoof
turning pure white as the blacksmith pared and trimmed,
leaving the nervous diamond of the frog well alone
but showing me,
just by looking,
how even to touch that,
much worse cut it,
would wake her
and break the spell
and our two heads with it.

Our collie dog sat near where the snake had been,
ravenous black and white,
all ears,
sometimes fidgeting her two slim front feet,
glancing away as if about to dash off,
then twisting back,
licking her lips and swallowing with a half-whine.

She knew better than to get under anyone's feet,
but when the blacksmith had done with his cutting,
and offered a new shoe,
and fiddled it downwards or sideways,
and hammered it with quick hits
which drove the nail-points clean through
(but these could be filed off later, and were)—
when this was all done,
he kicked the clippings across the cement
and now it was the collie's turn to show a sad restraint,
taking one delicate piece between her pink lips,
ashamed to be a slave of appetite,

and curving away into the yard
to eat it in private.

The blacksmith straightened himself,
one hand smoothing the small of his back,
the other picking a few remaining nails
from between his own darker lips,
then slapped Serenade on the flank with his red palm,
rousing her from her trance,
running his fingers up her mane and over her ears,

giving each a soft tug
and saying 'She'll do',
or 'Good lady',
or 'There's a girl.'

Whereupon my mother herself appeared to pay him—
their hands met, and touched, and parted,
and something passed between them—
and the blacksmith took off his apron
with its colours of a battered tin bowl,
folded it,
and carried it before him in a lordly fashion,
using it as a cushion for his collapsed bag
of hammers, clippers, knives, files, pliers and nails
to the van
which he had parked in the lane some distance from us,
while my mother untied the halter
and led her horse away.

There was a crisp clip-clop over the stable yard,
and a train of hoof-prints

with the neat shoes obvious to me,
who had stayed behind
with nothing better to do than look.

This was Serenade,
who would later throw my mother
as they jumped out of a wood into sunlight,
and who, taking all possible pains not to trample her down
or even touch her,
was nevertheless the means to an end,
which was death.

Now I am as old as my mother was then,
at the time of her fall,
and I can see Serenade clearly in her own later life,
poor dumb creature nobody blamed,
or could easily like any more either,
which meant nobody came to talk to her much
in the spot she eventually found
under the spiky may tree in the field,
and still less came to shoe her,
so her hooves grew long and crinkled round the edges
like wet cardboard (except they were hard)

while she just stood there,
not knowing what she had done,
or went off with her girlish flounce and conker-coloured arse,
waiting for something important to happen,
only nothing ever did,
beyond the next day and the next,
and one thing leading to another.

CLOSE

I pull back the curtain
and what do I see
but my wife on a sheet
and the screen beside her
showing our twins
out of their capsule
in mooning blue,
their dawdlers' legs
kicking through silence
enormously slowly,
while blotches beneath them
revolve like the earth
which will bring them to grief
or into their own.

I pull back the curtain
and what do I see
but my mother asleep,
or at least not awake,
and the sheet folded down
to show me her throat
with its wrinkled hole
and the tube inside
which leads to oxygen
stashed round her bed,
as though any day now
she might lift into space
and never return
to breathe our air.

I pull back the curtain
and what do I see
but the stars in the sky,
and their jittery light
stabbing through heaven
jabs me awake
from my dream that time
will last long enough
and let me die happy,
not yearning for more
like a man lost in space
might howl for the earth,
or a dog for the moon
with no reason at all.

A BLOW TO THE HEAD

On the Metro,
two stops in from Charles de Gaulle,
somebody slapped my wife.

Just like that—
a gang of kids—
for moving her bag
from the seat to her lap:
a thunderclap
behind my back.

Very next thing
was reeling dark
and the kids outside
beside themselves:
You didn't see!
You didn't see!
It might be him!
It wasn't me!

For the rest,
she wept through every station into Paris,
her head on my shoulder like love at the start of its life.

|||||||||||

By the merest chance
I had in mind
J. K. Stephen

who damaged his head
in Felixstowe (Suffolk)
in '86.

The nature of the accident is not certainly known;
in the Stephen family it was said he was struck
by some projection from a moving train.

Not a serious blow,
but it drove him mad
(molesting bread
with the point of a sword;
seized with genius—
painting all night),

and finally killed him
as well as his father,
who two years later
surrendered his heart
with a definite crack,
like a sla . . .

||||||||||||

. . . which reminds me.
When I was a kid
a man called Morris
slapped my face
so crazily hard
he opened a room
inside my skull

where plates of light
skittered and slid
and wouldn't quite
fit, as they were meant to,
together.

It felt like the way,
when you stand between mirrors,
the slab of your face

shoots backwards and forwards
for ever and ever
with tiny delays,
so if you could only
keep everything still
and look to the end
of the sad succession,
time would run out
and you'd see yourself dead.

||||||||||||

There is an attic flat
with views of lead
where moonlight rubs
its greasy cream,

and a serious bed
where now my wife
lies down at last
and curls asleep.

I fit myself
along her spine
but dare not touch
her breaking skull,

and find my mother
returns to me
as if she was climbing
out of a well:

ginger with bruises,
hair shaved off,
her spongy crown
is ripe with blood.

I cover my face
and remember a dog
in the reeking yard
when the kid I was

came up to talk.
I was holding a choc
in my folded fist
but the dog couldn't tell

and twitched away,
its snivelling whine
like human fear,
its threadbare head

too crankily sunk
to meet my eye
or see what I meant
by my opening hand.

JUDGEMENT

I was raking leaves in the front bed
when a helicopter wittered overhead

and I saw the blindness of a clear lake
when a waterbug paddles the far light.

My happiness went. I had thought of death
and everything that desecrates the earth.

I had watched the blood of my children
spill, and the stones at my feet crack open.

I had slithered so far into the underlying mud
I even flung out a hand for the hand of God.

ıııııııııı

Other times
I am underground:
at dead of night
when green minutes
drip from the clock
and wear me down
to the sort of bone
a scavenger cur
picks out of muck
and buries later
but clean forgets,
so the years pass,

and the earth shifts,
and the bone turns
into nothing at all
like bone, or me,

or a single thing
waiting for light
and what it shows
of someone else
who lies awake
all night beside me
and never speaks.

⁣⁣⁣⁣⁣⁣⁣⁣⁣⁣⁣⁣

For the first time in years
I am on my knees

in the sweet savour
of incense and soap.

The hand of God
is a burst of sun

torn through the head
of a window-saint;

the voice of God
is a fly in a web.

They are lost to me.
I shut my eyes

and imagine a bed
overlooking a garden:

knee-high grass
and hysterical roses.

The day's almost done
and there's mist coming on.

An apple tree
by the furthest hedge

has the look of my wife
when her back is turned

and her head in her hands.
The best thing on earth

is to call her and ask
for a drink of water.

I call and call:
the kitchen tap;

a drink of water;
a drink of water

to taste and be sure
I am dying at home.

A GLASS OF WINE

Exactly as the setting sun
clips the heel of the garden,

exactly as a pigeon
roosting tries to sing
and ends up moaning,

exactly as the ping
of someone's automatic car-lock
dies into a flock
of tiny echo aftershocks,

a shapely hand of cloud
emerges from the crowd
of airy nothing that the wind allowed
to tumble over us all day
and points the way

towards its own decay,
but not before
a final sunlight-shudder pours
away across our garden floor

so steadily, so slow,
it shows you everything you need to know
about this glass I'm holding out to you,

its white, unblinking eye
enough to bear the whole weight of the sky.

THE FOX PROVIDES FOR HIMSELF

It could have been an afternoon at the end of our lives:
the children gone, the house quiet, and time our own.
Without a word, we stalled at a window looking down.

Weak winter sunlight sank through the beech tree next door,
skimming the top of our dividing wall, spilling a primrose
                                                    stain
surprisingly far into our own patch. Earlier that same year

we had laid new grass, and squares of earth underneath
                                                    it all
still showed like the pavement of an abandoned town,
though the grass itself had done well, and from that angle

looked white as the breeze admired it, while we simply
went on standing there, holding hands now, trying to drown
the faint dynamo hum of London and lift off into nowhere.

Maybe we did drift a little. At any rate, something changed:
a shadow worked itself loose at the edge of our world.
Not a shadow. A fox. We saw it droop over the neighbouring
                                                    wall

and step—using the sun as a plank of solid wood—
down through the air until, landing on all fours, it rolled
sideways (this was no stumble) and stretched out owning the
                                                    place.

Big for a fox, I thought, but said nothing, holding my breath,
the sun burning so far into his coat each bristle stood
distinct, ginger everywhere but in fact red rising through brown

to black, to grey at the tip, like bare plant stalks dying
towards the light, but of course soft, so I knew my hand
would come away warm if I touched and smelling of garlic.

First he just lay there checking the silent earth with one ear,
but soon the music started and he was up—a puppet
living a secret life, stiff-spined but getting the hang of it,

doing everything he had seen real foxes do and not been able,
examining leaves, staring out flowers, then deciding to stop that,
there was no danger here, only pleasure, and to prove it he must

fold his dainty front paws, stick his ramrod brush in the air,
angle his plough-shaped mask to the grass, keep his back legs
normal, and shunt himself slowly forward inch by inch,

left cheek, then right, then left, then right again,
smearing his mouth so far open I saw the pegs
of his teeth—the pink inside the gums flecked with black—

before he tired of that too, and found under our laurel bush
the children's football, a sorry pink and blue punctured thing
which must be killed now, now, and in one particular way—

by flicking it smartly into the air and, as it fell,
butting it almost too far to reach but hoiking it back
on invisible strings, bringing death down in a frenzy

of grins and delirious yaps. After that, silence again.
When I returned to myself the fox was upright,
his coat convulsed in an all-over shrug

as if it were new and not fitting, like a dog when it jumps
out of water and stands legs braced in a halo of dew,
before trotting off in a hurry once more, which soon he did,

back to the neighbour's wall, and as he leaped he seemed
to hang on the bricks for a moment, slackened as though
his skeleton slipped from his body, or so I thought,

watching the breeze re-open his fur, and waiting to see
how he dropped—hardly a fox now, more like a trickle of rust—
my hand holding your hand as he went, then letting go.

ON THE ISLAND

The intricate and lovely yacht we saw
was due to go,
that last night lay far out
and caught the sunset like a silver seed,

today has gone indeed
and left the skyline bare without a doubt,
except to show
we cannot think it saw us any more.

FOOTSTEPS

for Richard Holmes

I set my course south-east, and go to find
the Margate where John Keats—audacious, well,
and braced to catch the moment that his mind
became itself—hired lodgings like the swell
he never was, just off the central square—
then take the narrow track through wheat fields on
towards the 'clift' (his word) and silence where
he saw Apollo step down from the sun.

I never got there. As I spun my way
through Kent, across the marshes, fog rolled in
so fast and penny-brown I went astray.
A gauzy church came next. Some graves. And then
a man in irons crouching by a stone,
exhausted, bloody-faced, and not alone.

THE BALCONY

The other, smaller islands we can see
by turning sideways on our balcony—

the bubble-pods and cones, the flecks of green,
the basalt-prongs, the moles, the lumpy chains—

were all volcanoes once, though none so tall
and full of rage of life as ours, which still

displays its flag of supple wind-stirred smoke
as proof that one day soon it will awake

again and wave its twizzle-stick of fire,
demolish woods, block roads, consume entire

communities with stinking lava-slews
which seem too prehistoric to be true

but are. Or will be. For today we sit
and feel what happiness the world permits.

The metal sun hangs still, its shadows fixed
and permanent. The sea-smell mixed

with thyme and oleander throws a drape
insidious as mist across the drop

of roofs and aerials, of jigsaw squares,
of terraced streets side-stepping to the shore,

or bathers sprawling on their stones, of waves
like other bathers turning in their graves,

and there, beyond them in the blistered shade
below the mountain, of the clumsy bird—

no, bi-plane, with a bucket slung beneath—
which sidles idly in to drench a wreath

of bush-fire in the fields, a fire that we
suppose means nothing to us here, but have to see.

A DUTCH INTERIOR

The dogs are a serious bore—
the pointer and the spaniel.
Their nails on the check floor
set painfully on edge
the teeth of each and everyone:
that stiffly-standing page,

that dutiful and downcast girl,
and most of all that woman who
has recently uncurled
a message from its ribbon-ring,
read it through, and now feels
all her strength departing.

A freshly-whitewashed wall
behind her takes the weight;
stern morning sunlight pulls
her shadow to the dot of noon;
everything about her starts
then stops again.

The dogs, however, they
already know. See that one there,
the pointer? Just the way
he crouches shows he's lost the will
to fight. The path is clear
and sweetly open for the spaniel.

MYTHOLOGY

31 August 1997

Earth's axle creaks; the year jolts on; the trees
begin to slip their brittle leaves, their flakes of rust;
and darkness takes the edge off daylight, not
because it wants to—never that. Because it must.

And you? Your life was not your own to keep
or lose. Beside the river, swerving underground,
the future tracked you, snapping at your heels:
Diana, breathless, hunted by your own quick hounds.

PASSING ON

By noon your breathing had changed from normal
to shallow and panicky. That's when the nurse said
Nearly there now, in the gentle voice of a parent
comforting a child used to failure, slipping her arms
beneath your shoulders to hoist you up the pillows,
then pressing a startling gauze pad under your jaw.

Nearly there now. The whole world seemed to agree—
as the late April sky deepened through the afternoon
into high August blue, the vapour trails of two planes
converged to sketch a cross on the brow of heaven.
My brother Kit and I kept our backs turned to that
except now and again. It was the room I wanted to see,

because it contained your last example of everything:
the broken metal window-catch that meant no fresh air;
your toothbrush standing to attention in its plastic mug;
the neutral pink walls flushed into definite pale red
by sunlight rejoicing in the flowering cherry outside;
your dressing-gown like a stranger within the wardrobe

eavesdropping. That should have been a sign to warn us,
but unhappiness made us brave, or do I mean cowardly,
and Kit and I talked as if we were already quite certain
you could no longer hear us, saying how easy you were
to love, but how difficult always to satisfy and relax—
how impossible to talk to, in fact, how expert with silence.

You breathed more easily by the time we were done,
although the thought you might have heard us after all,
and our words be settling into your soft brain like stones
onto the bed of a stream—that made our own breathing
tighter. Then the nurse looked in: *Nothing will change*
here for a while boys, and we ducked out like criminals.

I was ordering two large gins in the pub half a mile off
when my mobile rang. It was the hospital. You had died.
I put my drink down, then thought again and finished it.
Five minutes later we were back at the door of your room
wondering whether to knock. Would everything we said
be written on your face, like the white cross on the heavens?

Of course not. It was written in us, where no one could find it
except ourselves. Your own face was wiped entirely clean—
and so, with your particular worries solved, and your sadness,
I could see more clearly than ever how like mine it was,
and therefore how my head will eventually look on the pillow
when the wall opens behind me, and I depart with my failings.

THE MOWER

With storm light in the east but no rain yet
I came in from mowing my square of lawn
and paused in the doorway to glance round
at my handiwork and the feckless apple blossom

blurring those trim stripes and Hover-sweeps
I had meant to last. What I saw instead was you
in threadbare cords, catching the sunny interval
between showers, trundling the Ransome out

from its corner in the woodshed. The dizzy whiff
of elm chips and oil. Joke-shop spider-threads
greying the rubber handles. Gravel pips squeaking
as the roller squashed through the yard. Then a hush

like the pause before thunder while you performed
your ritual of muffled curses and forehead wipes,
your pessimistic tugs on the starter cable,
more curses, more furious heaves, until at long last

the engine sulked, recovered, sighed a grey cloud
speckled with petrol-bits, and wobbled into a roar.
Off came the brake and off charged the machine,
dragging you down to the blazing Tree of Heaven

at the garden end, where the trick was to reverse
without stalling or scraping a hefty mud-crescent,
before you careered back towards Kit and me
at our place in the kitchen window, out of your way.

To and fro, to and fro, to and fro, to and fro,
and each time a few feet more to the left, sometimes
lifting one hand in a hasty wave which said *Stay put!*
but also *I'm in charge!*, although we understood

from the way your whole body lurched lopsided
on the turn, this was less than a hundred percent true.
Getting the job done was all we ever wanted,
parked with our cricket things and happy enough

to wait, since experience had taught us that after
you'd unhooked the big green metal grass-basket
with its peeling By Royal Appointment transfer,
lugged it off to the smoking heap by the compost,

thumped it empty, then re-appeared to give us
the thumbs up, we were allowed to burst suddenly
out like dogs into the sweet air, measure the pitch
between our studious stump-plantings, toss to see

who went in first, then wait for you to turn up again
from the woodshed where you had taken five minutes
to switch the petrol off, and wipe the blades down,
and polish the grass basket although it never would

shine up much, being what you called venerable.
You always did come back, that was the thing.
As you also come back now in the week you died,
just missing the first thick gusts of rain and the last

of the giddy apple blossoms falling into your footprints,
with bright grass-flecks on your shoes and trouser-legs,
carefree for the minute, and young, and fit for life,
but cutting clean through me then vanishing for good.

II

LAURELS AND DONKEYS

(2009–2015)

A MOMENT OF REFLECTION

28 June 1914

Although an assassin has tried
and failed to blow him to pieces earlier this morning,
Archduke Ferdinand has let it be known
he will very soon complete his journey
as planned along the quay in Sarajevo.

For a moment, however,
he has paused to recover his composure
at the window of a private room in the Town Hall,
after finding the blood of his aide-de-camp
spattered over the manuscript of the speech
he was previously unable to complete.

And indeed,
the prospect of an Austrian brewery in the distance
is reassuring,
likewise the handsome bulk of the barracks
filled with several thousand soldiers of the fatherland.

This is how those who survive today will remember him:

a man thinking his thoughts
until his wife has finished her duties—
the Countess Chotek, with her pinched yet puddingy features,
to whom he will whisper shortly,
'Sophie, live for our children',
although she will not hear.

As for his own memories:

the Head of the local Tourist Bureau has now arrived
and taken it upon himself to suggest
the Archduke might be happy to recall the fact
that only last week he bagged his three thousandth stag.

Was this, the Head dares to enquire,
with the double-barrelled Mannlicher
made for him especially—
the same weapon he used to dispatch
two thousand one hundred and fifty game birds
in a single day,
and sixty boars in a hunt led by the Kaiser?

These are remarkable achievements
the Head continues,
on the same level as the improvement
the Archduke has suggested in the hunting of hare,
by which the beaters,
forming themselves into a wedge-shape,
squeeze those notoriously elusive creatures
towards a particular spot
where he can exceed the tally of every other gun.

In the silence that follows
it is not obvious whether the Archduke
has heard the question.

He has heard it.

He is more interested, however,
in what these questions bring to mind:

an almost infinite number of woodcock,
pigeon, quail, pheasant and partridge,
wild boars bristling flank to flank,
mallard and teal and geese
dangling from the antlers of stags,
layer after layer of rabbits
and other creatures that are mere vermin—

a haul that he predicts will increase
once the business of today has been completed.

SETTING THE SCENE

Before I come to the trenches, let me tell you the village
is a ruin and the church spire a stump; every single house
has been devastated by shell-bursts and machine-gun fire.

I saw a hare advance down the main street a moment ago,
then pause with the sun shining bright red through his ears.

LAURELS AND DONKEYS

Afterwards, when everyone who suddenly burst out singing
has stopped again, Siegfried Sassoon settles back into the haze

of the old century. It is 1897, he is 11, and this is Edingthorpe
in north Norfolk. His mother, wearing her light purple cloak,

has packed herself with the wicker picnic basket, bathing gear,
and three sons into the long shandrydan, drawn by a donkey,

which has been led round from the Rectory by the gardener.
There is a plan to take a dip in the river but, as the expedition

begins, Emily Eyles appears on the doorstep exclaiming
Madam has left without her sunshade after all. No matter.

When everything is quiet again, she closes it with a neat click
and the faintest creak of collapsing silk, then traipses indoors

where she falls to thinking about Mr Dawson, her young man,
who has saved for long enough to open his shop in the village

when they are married next year. 'White wings that never weary'
she sings, washing up cups and dishes. By now the little party

has reached the village church, where the years become confused.
Siegfried clambers down without the others noticing, and leans

his leather elbows on the lych gate. The carved gold lettering says
it was built when the war ended, in memory of a lance-corporal

whose father was rector here for 19 years and is buried nearby,
although the boy himself, having fought at Mons, Le Cateau,

the Arne, the Aisne, The First Battle of Ypres and at Hill 60,
drowned in the Transport *Royal Edward* crossing the Aegean Sea

on 13 August 1915. By peculiar chance it is 13 August today,
and in a moment Siegfried's younger brother will also be buried

at sea, after receiving a mortal wound on the Gallipoli Peninsula.
'Don't let the donkey eat the laurel' their mother tells the children;

she knows it is poisonous. Laurels and donkeys. Siegfried agrees
but will not ruin his afternoon, so picks a poppy and a cornflower,

lays them on the ground beside the lych gate, then turns placidly
down the farm lane, over the style, and along the path that leads

through the meadow to the Rectory garden, and so to the river,
where in another short minute or two the others find him waiting.

AN EQUAL VOICE

We hear more from doctors than patients. However hard he tries, the historian cannot even the account, cannot give the patients an equal voice, because most of them chose not to recount their experiences.

—A War of Nerves, *by Ben Shephard*

War from behind the lines is a dizzy jumble.
Revolving chairs, stuffy offices, dry-as-dust
reports, blueprints one day and the next—
with the help of a broken-down motor car
and a few gallons of petrol—marching men
with sweat-stained faces and shining eyes,
horses straining and plunging at the guns,
white sweat-clouds drifting beneath them,
and piles of bloody clothes and leggings
outside the canvas door of a field hospital.
At the end of the week there is no telling
whether you spent Tuesday going over
the specifications of a possible laundry
or skirting the edge of hell in an automobile.

|||||||||||||||

There were some cases of nervous collapse
as the whistle blew on the first day of battle.
In general however it is perfectly astonishing
and terrifying how bravely the men fight.
From my position on rising ground I watched
one entire brigade advancing in line after line,
dressed as smartly as if they were on parade,

and not a single man shirked going through
the barrage, or facing the rapid machine-gun
and rifle-fire that finally wiped them out.
I saw with my own eyes the lines advancing
in such admirable order quickly melt away.
Yet not a man wavered, or broke the ranks
or made any attempt to turn back again.

|||||||||||

A soft siffle, high in the air like a distant lark,
or the note of a penny whistle, faint and falling.
But then, with a spiral, pulsing flutter, it grew
to a hissing whirr, landing with ferocious blasts,
followed by the whine of fragments that cut
into the trees, driving white scars into their trunks
and filling the air with torn shreds of foliage.
The detonation, the flash, the heat of explosion.
And all the while fear, crawling into my heart.
I felt it. Crawling into me. I had to set my teeth
and steadied myself, but to no avail. I clutched
the earth, pressing against it. There was no one
to help me then. O how one loves mother earth.

|||||||||||

One or two friends stood like granite rocks
round which the seas raged, but very many
other men broke in pieces. Everyone called it
shell-shock, meaning concussion. But shell-
shock is rare. What 90 percent get is justifiable
funk due to the collapse of their self-control.

You understand what you see but cannot think.
Your head is in agony and you want relief for that.
The more you struggle, the more madness creeps
over you. The brain cannot think of anything at all.
I don't ask you what you feel like but I tell you
because I have been like you. I have been ill as you
and got better. I will teach you, you will get better.
Try and keep on trying what I tell you and you will.

||||||||||||

The place was full of men whose slumbers were morbid,
titubating shell-shockers with their bizarre paralyses
and stares, their stammers and tremors, their nightmares
and hallucinations, their unstoppable fits and shakings.
Each was back in his doomed shelter, when the panic
and stampede was re-enacted among long-dead faces,
or still caught in the open and under fire. This officer
was quietly feasting with imaginary knives and forks;
that group roamed around clutching teddy bears;
one man stripped to his underclothes and proclaimed
himself to be Mahatma Gandhi; another sat cramped
in a corner clutching a champagne cork; one chanted,
with his hands over an imaginary basket of eggs, Lord
have mercy on us, Christ have mercy, Lord have mercy.

||||||||||||

I could feel the bullets hit my body. I could feel
myself being hit by gunfire and this is what made me
sit up and scream. What I saw round me were others
walking with the bent and contorted spines of old age,

or moving without lifting their legs but vibrating them
on the ground. All equally unfortunate, filled with sadness.
Dead friends gazed at them. Rats emerged from the cavities
of bodies. Then trembling began, and losing control of legs:
you never dreamt of such gaits. One fellow cannot hold
his head still or even stand except with incessant jerking.
Instantly the man across the aisle follows suit. In this way
the infection spreads in widening circles until the whole
ward is jerking and twitching, all in their hospital blues,
their limbs shaking and flapping like the tails of dogs.

|||||||||||

Naturally it can save a good deal of time if men,
before battle, have pictures from the Hate Room hung
in their minds of things the enemy have already done,
waiting to be remembered. Starving people for instance
and sick people and dead people in ones and heaps,
with bodies all bearing witness to hideous cruelties.
Compulsory mourning is no longer recommended
whereby the hospital confines a man for three days
alone in a darkened room and orders him to grieve
for dead comrades. But other cures must be attempted,
and in some cases men even wish to return to their duty.
See, your eyes are already heavy. Heavier and heavier.
You are going into a deep, deep sleep. A deep, far sleep.
You are far asleep. You are fast asleep. You have no fear.

|||||||||||

I am quiet and healthy but cannot bear being away
from England. I have been away too long and seen
too many things. My best friend was killed beside me,
I have a wife and two children, and I have done enough.
I thought my nerves were better but they are worse.
The first fight, the fight with my own self, had ended.
I may be ready to fight again but I am not willing.
I am in urgent need of outdoor work and would be glad
to accept a position as a gamekeeper at a nominal salary.
My best friend walked back into my room this morning,
shimmering white and transparent. I saw him clearly.
He stood at the foot of my bed and looked right at me.
I asked him, What do you want? What do you want?
Eventually I woke up and of course I was by myself.

THE LIFE OF HARRY PATCH

'The Last Fighting Tommy'

1.

A curve is a straight line caught bending
and this one runs under the kitchen window
where the bright eyes of your mum and dad
might flash any minute and find you down
on all fours, stomach hard to the ground,
slinking along a furrow between the potatoes
and dead set on a prospect of rich pickings,
the good apple trees and plum trees and pears,
anything sweet and juicy you might now be
able to nibble round the back and leave
hanging as though nothing had touched it,
if only it were possible to stand upright
in so much clear light with those eyes
beady in the window and not catch a packet.

2.

Patch, Harry Patch, that's a good name,
Shakespearean, it might be one of Hal's men
at Agincourt or not far off, although in fact
it starts life and belongs in Combe Down
with your dad's trade in the canary limestone
which turns to grey and hardens when it meets
the light, perfect for Regency Bath and you too
since no one these days thinks about the danger
of playing in quarries when the workmen go,
not even of prodding and pelting with stones
the wasps' nests perched on rough ledges
or dropped down from the ceiling on stalks
although god knows it means having to shift
tout de suite and still get stung on arms and faces.

3.

First the hard facts of not wanting to fight,
and the kindness of deciding to shoot men
in the legs but no higher unless needs must,
and the liking among comrades which is truly
as deep as love without that particular name,
then Pilckem Ridge and Langemarck and across
the Steenbeek since none of the above can change
what comes next, which is a lad from A Company
shrapnel has ripped open from shoulder to waist
who begs you 'Shoot me', but is good as dead
already, and whose final word is 'Mother',
which you hear because you kneel a minute,
hold one finger of his hand, then remember orders
to keep pressing on, support the infantry ahead.

4.

After the beautiful crowd to unveil the memorial
and no puff in the lungs to sing 'O Valiant Hearts'
or say aloud the names of friends and one cousin,
the butcher and chimney sweep, a farmer, a carpenter,
work comes up the Wills Tower in Bristol and there
thunderstorms are a danger, so bad that lightning
one day hammers Great George and knocks down
the foreman who can't use his hand three weeks
later as you recall, along with the way that strike
burned all trace of oxygen from the air, it must have,
given the definite stink of sulphur and a second
or two later the shy wave of a breeze returning
along with rooftops below, and moss, and rain
fading the green Mendip Hills and blue Severn.

5.

You grow a moustache, check the mirror, notice
you're forty years old, then next day shave it off,
check the mirror again—and find you're seventy,
but life is like that now, suddenly and gradually
everyone you know dies and still comes to visit
or you head back to them, it's not clear which
only where it happens: a safe bedroom upstairs
on the face of it, although when you sit late
whispering with the other boys in the Lewis team,
smoking your pipe upside-down to hide the fire,
and the nurses on night duty bring folded sheets
to store in the linen cupboard opposite, all it takes
is someone switching on the light—there is that flash,
or was until you said, and the staff blacked the window.

THE DEATH OF HARRY PATCH

When the next morning eventually breaks,
a young Captain climbs onto the fire step,
knocks ash from his pipe then drops it
still warm into his pocket, checks his watch,
and places the whistle back between his lips.

At 06.00 hours precisely he gives the signal,
but today nothing that happens next happens
according to plan. A very long and gentle note
wanders away from him over the ruined ground
and hundreds of thousands of dead who lie there

immediately rise up, straightening their tunics
before falling in as they used to do, shoulder
to shoulder, eyes front. They have left a space
for the last recruit of all to join them: Harry Patch,
one hundred and eleven years old, but this is him

now, running quick-sharp along the duckboards.
When he has taken his place, and the whole company
are settled at last, their padre appears out of nowhere,
pausing a moment in front of each and every one
to slip a wafer of dry mud onto their tongues.

RHAPSODY

In Memory of George Butterworth

George Butterworth whose name meant nothing to me
those five years I biked up and down my school drive
under chestnuts bare or flaunting their big candelabras
past the lodge where he wrote 'The Banks of Green Willow'.

The same George Butterworth who today I encounter
on YouTube dancing a folk medley at Burford in 1913
sporting white flannels, white handkerchief, knee-bells
and drooping moustache before these things turned quaint.

George Butterworth who three years later was shot dead
not ducking low enough in his trench and whose melodies
now will never stop pouring out over the wire and mud
where he lay down in his dark uniform his darkened head.

IN THE STACKS

1.

These dry scraps are five olive leaves
Denis Browne pulled from the olive tree
growing above the grave he had just dug

on Skyros for Rupert Brooke in April 1915
and posted back home to Cathleen Nesbitt.
They lie here as brittle and glittering now

as the scales of a surprisingly large fish,
but I think they are what it says they are,
because strange as it may seem I myself

stood under the same tree fifty years later,
aged 17 and so beginning to work out how
my life might be measured and must end,

thanks in part to the procession of red ants
marching from a narrow crack in the coping
designed for the grave by Brooke's mother

after Denis Browne had made his farewell
and boarded his ship the *Grantully Castle*,
sailing towards his own death at Gallipoli.

2.

Resting in his trench now but this soldier
with his soft cap and kilt, his bare knees
and open wind-nipped face, will disappear

over the top in a moment and so leave behind
the terrier, the jaunty white terrier called Argos
who, if his master returns, will raise his head

because this man smells like the same man
that left all those minutes ago, although to see
the changes in him now no one would think so.

3.

What flew in from another land
filled up the sky above the Strand—

an insect like a huge cigar
splashed about with tongues of fire,

with someone crouching at a door
despite our guns' tremendous roar

to drop his load of shiny bombs
across our dark and quiet homes.

Remember, I was still a child
and never thought I might be killed.

I liked the bombs, I liked the fire,
I liked the huge high-up cigar,

I liked especially how the lights
cut misty pathways through the night

and how my footsteps made no sound
when I walked there, not on the ground.

4.

This report is a continuation of one numbered 303A
and contains extracts of letters from Indian soldiers
relating to the fortnight concluded on 13th inst.
Those cited here illustrate how almost impossible it is
for barriers to be effective in Oriental correspondence.

Among several examples showing courage and duty
Orientals excel in the art of conveying their information
without saying anything definite (*words missing here*).
When they have meaning to convey they are apt to use
a phrase such as 'Think it over until you understand it',
or some equivalent. It naturally follows that their news
is exceedingly vague and will give rise to wild rumours.

It has nevertheless been possible to draw some conclusions;
eg: the prospect of a return to the firing line appears to be
regarded with something approaching (*words missing here*),
as in 'My brother, this is no war. It is the final destruction
of the world. A whole world is being killed. If ever I return
I shall tell you very much. If I end here, what is there to tell.'

In the same way, extracts show that the man who has served
and been wounded feels he has amply (*words missing here*),
as in: 'The guns are firing. The Kings are looking on. Like dust
the dead are lying before the trench. Thus are we all sacrificed.'

5.

What tree was felled in what remote forest,
then dragged by what engine or elephant
through what jungle to what paper-mill
in what sea-port, then shipped to what dock

then sold how and cut how and brought how
for 2nd Lieutenant Owen on this particular day
in Craiglockhart War Hospital in Edinburgh
to single it out thinking, Now, here, with this

pen on this table-top with this my right hand
I shall write these particular words in this order
to catch what I am trying to say then pass it
along the corridor to him who just happens

to be recovering there from his own troubles,
and who, when not practising his golf swing,
will read them and recommend that one thing
becomes another, for example the word 'dead'

which he thinks should be 'doomed', and also
that 'silent minds' be changed to 'patient minds'?

6.

At the very end of everything, the last man emerges
through a copse of trees without any leaves or branches
and comes to a halt on the greasy slope of a bomb crater

where in a brown puddle he sees his own face looking up
to remind him of the need to wash himself. Laying aside
on the pitted bank his tin hat and satchel, his lousy jacket,

he slithers forward as close as he dare to the water's edge
where mud immediately swallows his boots to the ankle,
spreads his legs while at the same time leaning forward

as if the air itself were solid enough to stop him toppling,
and scoops a dark handful from the pool. The impression,
as he uses his left hand to smear the water over his neck

and jaw, and his right to continue the process over his chin
and mouth, is of a man taking a firm grip of his own face
before twisting his head off the delicate screw of his neck

and rather than washing himself throwing away his skull
along with everything inside it that can never be forgotten
and so, at the very end of everything, become clean again.

BEYOND ALL CALCULATION

We left England before dawn, flying high and easy
across the Channel, then dropped into the worst of it
behind a farmhouse near Le Mesnil; forty or fifty men
were awaiting evacuation, so we dealt with them fast,

before hundreds of others began arriving from Gold Beach.
The yard was soon like the threshold of a slaughterhouse—
bloodstained uniforms, boots, caps and helmets and berets.
The interior of the kitchen and double-parlour is best left

to the imagination. Suffice it to say we would be kept busy
for three or four days straight through without any sleep,
but we had Benzedrine, and so did the stretcher-bearers—
willing but unseasoned boys who took it the hardest,

hesitating to lift their burdens unless they could turn
their backs. They became veterans that first morning.
Anyone would have done, watching the hands working,
seeing the orderlies giving blood, the wounds excised

then dressed as soon as the bleeding was under control
and limbs immobilised. When the break-out finally came,
with the men squeezed tight together in those deep lanes
and pressing towards the horizon, they saw cattle dead

in the grazing on every side, their legs stiff and straight up.
No one had milked them; it was something that had been
forgotten. In the silence afterwards, ambulances appeared.
We climbed into these with our equipment and followed on.

JOHN BUXTON

Captain John Buxton, a prisoner of the German army
for all five years of the Second World War, examined
with precision and devotion the life of the creatures
around him, then chose as his one particular subject
the redstart, a small bird that in continental Europe

usually prefers the surroundings of human habitation
but in Britain is a secretive devotee of the wood-edge.
It is clear from his work that leisure, especially if limited,
is very much better used in the study of a single species
than attempting a general and comprehensive survey.

He began as he meant to continue: *I must be understood*
to refer only to my redstarts. My redstarts? The chief joy
of watching them is to prove they inhabit another world.
He ended as he began, after eight hundred and fifty hours
scrutinising a single pair between April and June 1943

near the left bank of the river Altmühl where it flows
through the former valley of the Danube near Eichstätt.
Although no pair of birds has ever been watched so closely,
I feel that I know only a little of these strange creatures,
merrily busking about the pine trees that shaded some

two thousand of us, or perching on the wires that kept us
close. Their pink and silvery wings. The fragile pattern
of their songs and the ethereal sweetness of their actions.
What matters is: the redstarts lived where I could see them,
untroubled all day long except by their own necessities.

MATINEE IDOL

Hello Mother you will remember I always wanted
to be a movie star. Now they have encouraged us

to make this and promise it will be shown widely
in the cinemas at home. Funny how things turn out.

I am well as you see and no small thanks to your cake—
the other fellows were very glad to share that with me.

Give my regards to Father and also to Nancy. Tell her
not to worry. I am well as you see. Also give my best

to Uncle Eric and Aunt Betty, Steve, and everyone else
at the White Hart. To everyone you can think of in fact.

Tell them not to worry about me. I am well as you see
and will be home quite soon with everything forgotten.

That's my time up, so I shall say good-bye for the moment.
Here is Corporal Wagstaff with a message for his mother.

CHANGI

For the funeral of Miss Jackson, a retired missionary
of the Methodist mission, our congregation was joined
by some from the women's camp. This was the first time

I had been part of a mixed group since captivity began
three years before, and hearing the voices of these women
I turned aside to inspect a troop of small yellow flowers

under a grove of rubber trees. I had never seen this plant
before coming to the Sime Road Camp. So far as I knew
it was the only species of wild flower to flourish there

in short turf, like the crocus at home. It had a green stalk
a foot high, and a head of three petals folded into a bulb.
I thought it must be an iris and have since confirmed that.

THE STATION AT VITEBSK

Our town stood on the extreme limit of the world.
At the railway station, all the trains that drew up
to Platform One were returning home to Vitebsk,
and all the trains at Platform Two were leaving

Vitebsk. We swung between hello and good-bye
like the long brass pendulum of the station clock
that never helped me answer my question: were we
living at the beginning of the world or the end of it?

The waiting-room had a ceiling painted blue and gold
but the atmosphere was always tense with anxiety—
everyone was preparing to leave for somewhere else.
They might hear the bell ring three times and still

have to watch their train disappear into the distance
without them: the destination had not been announced.
All they could do then was settle down to wait again,
as if next time the Messiah would finally show himself.

My beautiful train roared, the boiler gulped flames,
and steam swallowed truck after truck of passengers.
We were travelling at last, losing the town in a cloud.
I felt I might have been going home after a funeral,

or setting out on my way to a funeral. Would there be
a place for me when I arrived, and faces I recognised?
Would the trees still be there—the deep forest I knew,
and used to feel breathing on me when I was a child?

COMING IN TO LAND

Twenty minutes out from Base
    we begin a glide on course
from ten thousand feet.

    Up here it is hot in the sun,
but we can see on the ground
    it will be dull.
Broken layers of stratocumulus
    are waste lands stretching
        as far as the horizon;
they are at two thousand,
and won't worry us for a while yet.

We live by death's negligence—
    I believe that,
and think of Don,
    though there is nothing to say;
falling short makes me despise myself.

With airspeed at 85 mph,
    the surging roar has ceased,
        and now the old kite rests on the air
slightly nose-down
        and sighing.

No vibration;
    both engines muted;
        the props meandering round

while the distant world imperceptibly approaches
with small clouds anchored like white Zeppelins
    and flashing lakes
        and river-bends beyond them.

I never realised how much my life involved him—
    things I remember are endless,
        the whole region seems loaded
          and rich with them:
Friesians lifting their heads from grazing;
    cottage washing lines;
        dust following a plough.

All these sights become
    more
        and less real over time.

Shall I see Jean when I'm home on leave?

    When Mrs P let me know
Don had volunteered for airborne work overseas
    I said 'Jean will be sorry',
        but 'Not sorry, proud'
          came the answer;
that soon brought me
    (betraying my own youth)
        to youth's error:
          what if he's killed?

Here we go,
    sinking over the road,

across the field,
skimming the hedge,
and straight to the beginning of the runway.

It flattens out;
it broadens;
it rises to become hard ground rushing past.

Our engines barely murmur,
but we still rest on the air
while grass streams away on either side.

At last comes the crunch of first contact.

We bounce a little
and bump again—

bump   (pause),
bump,
bump,
bump,
bump,
bump—
settling in quicker until we are easy.

A grand life.

Sooner or later
we shall come into line with the rest
and stop.

Then the engines will cut,
the props jerking stickily to a halt.

Then the silence will sing to me.

THE KOREAN MEMORIAL AT HIROSHIMA

There was hardly time
between the Peace Museum
and the bullet train to Tokyo,
but our hosts instructed the taxi
to find the Memorial to the Koreans.
Ten thousand Koreans, killed that morning.
You, being Korean, had to see it.

||||||||||||

We had been crying in the Museum:
the charred school uniforms;
the lunch-box with its meal of charcoal;
the shadow of a seated woman
printed on the steps of a bank.
Everyone else was crying too.
We shuffled round in a queue,
crying and saying nothing.

Then we stood in the rain
squaring up to the Memorial.
A spike of rusty flowers
and a tide-scum of dead cherry blossom.
Five or six miniature ceremonial costumes
made of folded paper and left to moulder.
Pink. Pink and custard yellow.
You could hardly leave soon enough.

||||||||||||

The taxi only just made it,
sputtering among black cherries
then stalling by the skeleton
of the one dome to survive the blast.

No need to worry about the train, though.
The trains in Japan run on time.

In two hours and fifteen minutes
we would see Mount Fuji,
cloud-cover permitting,
and the snow-cap like a handkerchief
draped over a tumbler of water
in the moment of suspense
before a magician taps his wand
and the tumbler disappears.

NOW THEN

It was not my war, but all the same
my father handed over the harness
of his Sam Browne for me to polish,
and his enormous boots. There was
no way I could ever make the toes
brighter than they were already.

||||||||||||

Years later I was riding a train south
from Gdansk to Warsaw at 4.00 A.M.
The pine forest swarmed beside me,
lit by the gentle glow of our carriages
and sometimes by devilish icy sparks
which flew from our wheels at points.

||||||||||||

Tell him about the smell, my mother said,
working hard on his buttons with Brasso
at the window-end of the kitchen table.
She meant the smell of Belsen, the first
my father had known of any such place.
He slowly shook his head. *I don't think so.*

||||||||||||

The forest lasted for miles. Miles and miles.
Then for a second I saw deep into the heart
of a clearing: there was this swine-herd
lolling against the wall of his pine cabin
wearing the helmet of a German soldier.
And pigs rootling in the husky moonlight.

|||||||||||||

Why not? my mother continued her polishing.
Surely the boy is old enough to know history?
My father sighed: *Now then, you know the reason.*
That ended it. I kept my eyes down and attention
fixed on the long face looming in his toe-caps,
convinced my efforts would never pass muster.

|||||||||||||

Eventually I slept, dreaming through what remained
of the great pine forest of Europe, while my father
pounded along in the dark outside my carriage.
At Warsaw he fell away from me, but not before
passing his boots through the window and asking
would I mind giving them a last quick once-over.

A PINE CONE

From the flagstone path that swerves
past one mass grave
shaped like a flat-topped Neolithic long-barrow

to the next mass grave,

and wanders too
beside free-standing headstones
bearing individual or family names,
Anne Frank's among them,
that cannot be placed exactly
where the bodies lie
but remember them,

I brought away a pine cone,
one of thousands darkening the ground.

I carried it home and placed it here
on my window-sill in the open air
and milder English sun.

Now its stiff woody elements,
brown with darker brown fringes,
have turned into a creature
with manifold silent mouths
all stretched open to their fullest extent.

When I pick it up
it is lighter than before,

almost weightless between my fingers
but rustling faintly as I revolve it,

taking me back to the tree that reared above me
with its baked and fissured trunk,

and the stone path I was halfway down,

and the graves I had passed
and those still to come
flattened under their gloss of flowering heather
and spirals of lark song.

Little one. Little
creature abandoned.
Tell me
what should I do next
with your useless beauty.

I breathe. I exclaim
when your brittle weight passes
from my hand onto the window sill again;

the breeze catches and rolls it,
threatening a fall,

then a moment later drifts idly away
and there you stay.

AFTER THE WAR

My father is in the Territorial Army planning a rearguard action.
On Salisbury Plain to be precise, the night before Annual Exercise,
with a gale blowing.

He is sharing his billet with Colonel Sidgewick, who fought beside
    him
in Normandy through the Falaise Gap, then across Germany into
    Berlin,
where they demobbed.

Reveille is at 05.00 and they should be asleep but the wind has
    other ideas,
accelerating over the Downs to make one last and particularly
    fierce assault
against their hut.

The blow knocks Colonel Sidgewick's glass eye off his bedside
    table,
which my father knows because he hears it hit the floor like a
    marble.
Whereupon the Colonel

searches under the bed until he finds it again, rolls it around his
    mouth
with a watery plopping noise, then screws it back into his
    eye-socket
and makes an apology.

IN NORMANDY

My father is confused. This is the bend in the lane
where Major Gosling on a recce for the regiment
found a Panzer tank blocking his way like an ogre
and, swivelling his eyes round to the back of his head,
reversed between these high stone walls at top speed.

It was Spring then but is Summer now, and the buds
of marigolds and buttercups in the fields on either side
have exploded in riotous jubilation. This is what puzzles
my father, turning on his heel just where the Panzer was
to hear the painful bee-buzz of the backwards engine

and see again how a bullet fired through the turret-slit
strikes the Major through the right leg below the knee
preventing him from driving, whereupon he stumbles out,
and hops a very long three miles back to find my father
and tells him everything he can expect to find ahead.

THE CAMP

Near the dog's leg turn of the lane down to the ponies' field,
skulking in summer among cow parsley and meadowsweet,
in winter with their streaked black corrugated walls laid bare,
were the half-dozen Nissen huts my father refused to mention.
A prisoner of war camp for Italian soldiers my mother told me,
but also part of the silence my father had brought back with him
ten years before from Germany which now could not be ended
although the reason for that was another thing he never gave up.
Why spoil an early morning stroll bringing halters for the ponies
so we could lead them home to the stable yard then saddle up?
What else could there possibly be on earth for us to talk about
that was more interesting than a blackbird calling in the hedge,
or the swarming hawthorn flowers that smelled faintly of drains,
or the rain cloud that he always said was only a clearing shower?

DEMOBBED

Sixty-odd years after the war ended my father returned
home. No one told me to expect him, and by the time
I reached the airport, crowds were already surrounding

the Arrivals Gate. When an especially loud cheer went up
something told me it might be him, and I made an effort
to push through and enquire. Sure enough there he was

with his square shoulders, ramrod back, and polished hair,
but wearing his city suit which surprised me, and at his side
my brother Kit. Kit obviously knew something I had missed.

In any case, they marched straight past me without so much
as blinking, while the crowd continued to cheer gratefully
and the brass band played Colonel Bogey, until my brother

wheeled aside and my father lowered his head to disappear
between those long yellow flaps that luggage goes through,
where I imagine he quite simply laid himself down and died.

THE MINISTER

We flew Passenger to Kuwait,
where our driver ferried us to the military zone—
they were boiling tea at the check-point
and waved us straight through.

The Freight Building, next to Military Departures,
was signposted in Arabic script with a translation
that read 'The Fright Building'.

By the time our gate opened
I was weighed down by armour,
and accustomed
to the American soldiers who milled round us lazily
but always called me 'Sir'.

Our Minister, a late substitute and our *raison d'être*,
was another matter.
'Fuck this' was his verdict on officials
who deemed our papers not in order,
and much else besides.

We wasted a day in the Meridian Hotel,
then next morning set off again for the airport.
The fourth approach-road our driver tried
was the one without a blockade.
'Fuck that as well.'

The planes are in constant use,
so when our Hercules landed,

the pilot left the engines running
while the ramp
(which I recognised from shots of coffins coming home)
slowly lowered

and stopped 18 inches from the ground.
It was a struggle to get on board,
what with my luggage and armour,
but I found my seat,
a narrow canvas bench,
next to a Major from 2 Para,
who helped me with my belts and ear plugs.

There were no announcements.
We taxied,
roared down the runway,
and an hour later were in Basra
to take on board an Iraqi general
and his American liaison officer.

Eventually we reached Baghdad and started to corkscrew,
dropping tin foil to confuse the heat-seeking SAM missiles
before making an exceedingly low landing.
When I jumped onto the tarmac
it crossed my mind I might break something,
but I bounced and walked on.

Soon the Minister caught up:
What the fuck were we going to do now?
Why the fuck were we waiting in the open?
Where the fuck was the Puma
that would take us to the embassy?

'Look over there', I said,
and a moment later we were lifting off again in a great hurry,
thrashing over the empty streets,
firing flares when the pilot received a message,
which turned out to be false,
that a missile had locked on to us,
and dipping close to the ground.

The roofs were wonderful,
but the Tigris a disappointing chalky brown.
The Minister certainly thought so.
'Looks like a fucking drain.'
The surface whipped into little peaks as we crossed,
and ahead lay our landing pad in the Green Zone.
We had arrived safely.

An hour later the Minister was in the bar
practising his billiards.
'Hi', he said,
when I approached with our schedule of meetings.
'Finally we seem to have got our fucking passports stamped.'

Then he bent forward and concentrated on a difficult pot.

LOSSES

General Petraeus, when the death-count of American troops
in Iraq was close to 3,800, said 'The truth is you never do get
used to losses. There is a kind of bad news vessel with holes,

and sometimes it drains, then it fills up, then it empties again'—
leaving, in this particular case, the residue of a long story
involving one soldier who, in the course of his street patrol,

tweaked the antenna on the TV in a bar hoping for baseball,
but found instead the snowy picture of men in a circle talking,
all apparently angry and perhaps Jihadists. They turned out to be

reciting poetry. 'My life', said the interpreter, 'is like a bag of flour
thrown through wind into empty thorn bushes'. Then 'No, no',
    he said,
correcting himself. 'Like dust in the wind. Like a hopeless man.'

OP. BILLY

We arrived at 05.30 in a bloody freezing Kabul Airport
with snow piled head-high either side of the runways,
then drove through town for ten minutes to ISAF HQ
where I had my first sighting of the actual Afghanistan.

This was people wandering across a dual-carriageway
and shepherds with flocks of straggly goats. Lots of goats.
I soon discovered we have a permanent goat detachment,
although at the time of writing, the elders from Sangin

have eaten the last residents. The Officer in Charge of Goats
(OiCoG) is presently in the process of resourcing more;
this operation, Op. Billy, is now a routine drill. The OiCoG
will drive to town in an armoured Land Rover with support

from associated personnel which, on reaching the bazaar,
takes up a defensive position around the livestock section.
The OiCoG then moves swiftly to the Goat Man and begins
negotiations. It is impossible to over-estimate the importance

of the local elders in dealing with troublesome provinces,
and so also of the need for a goat that finds their approval.
Fortunately the OiCoG is fully UN Goat Authority, Selection
and Screening (UNIGASAS) trained, and within a few minutes

he will turn a goat on its back and make a thorough assessment. Now that we have been compelled to forgo weekly camel racing we are keen to procure two goats to initiate a similar competition. Until that becomes possible, we make bets on the peak numbers

of diarrhoea and vomiting cases in camp. I have pitched for 75 but understand there are others who have gone as high as 140. Good-bye for now. I am off to Death Row where I hope to sleep soundly until 06.00 hours when morning prayers will wake me.

THE GOLDEN HOUR

After major trauma a certain percentage of victims will die
within the first ten to fifteen minutes. There is another peak
around the hour mark. And a third at the two-to-three-day mark,
due to complications. We are not able to do much about the men
that are going to die in the first ten to fifteen minutes, so instead
we look to keep them alive during what we call 'the golden hour'.

For instance: one patient I remember had been in a blast situation
with no visible injury but we were not ventilating very well at all.
I put two openings in both sides of his chest with a big scalpel blade;
then I could stick my fingers in, and knew his right lung was down
because I could not feel it. However, I was now releasing trapped air
and the lung came back. He had responded within the golden hour.

VALLON MEN

On the gently sloping hill behind Norton Manor barracks,
home to 40 Commando, three trees, one for each marine,
have already been dedicated to the memory of those killed

during their tour of Sangin in 2007–8. A week ago today,
in bright November sunshine, fourteen more were planted
to commemorate those killed during the last six months.

'It was a very hard tour', said Gavin Taylor, aged twenty-
eight and a father of three. 'We have lost a lot of friends.
And we have seen a lot of things that are not ideal.'

HOME FRONT

1.

Near the end of life in my own body
I slept in a grove of mulberry trees,
with a mattress of soft sandstone
and warm breeze for my blanket.

I knew then I had crossed the brook Cedron,
and imagined strangers' hands
gathering the leaves that sheltered me
to feed silkworm,
then silkworm themselves,
working their miracle of change.

Gethsemane.

I believe I said the word aloud,
and shortly afterwards
the earth was taken from me.

When I awoke again
I had reached as far as the unsteady glass
of my front door at home.
I could make out my wife
in pieces on the far side,
stopping in our hallway
before she came to answer.

2.

I knew we were in serious trouble
when I looked from the landing window
and saw the two of them together,
their hats showing above the front hedge.

Our boy saw as well and I called out:
Don't let them in.
But he thought it was Dad come back,
so ran downstairs
and when they knocked he opened anyway.

3.

It is difficult to imagine
how beautiful
a Hercules transport plane can appear to be
when cloud-cover breaks
and the home approach begins.

The engines, too:
they start like a rumour,
then become multitudes at prayer,
then a deep Amen.

A most beautiful sound.

He detested the rain all his life
although I adore it,
and was soaked through
the instant I took my place alongside him
in our procession across the tarmac.

Dry sand would still have been glittering in his hair.
and in the corners of his eyes, his ears,
more sand.

PEACE TALKS

1.

WAR DEBTS

I started
living with Debbie when I was fifteen,
but I was never the best-behaved boy in school
so obviously she had a bit of a battle there.

Then I went to college but I sacked that,

so my sister's boyfriend, he asked me
have you ever thought about joining the army,
and I told him
I've not, but I will now,
and next thing there I was
doing my Phase One at Purbright,
then Lark Hill—the rolling plains.

We knew,
right,
we knew we were going out,
and it was like,
guys,
this is going to be tough.

Did you know Camp Bastion is the size of Reading?
I didn't know.
And 95 degrees with your body armour.

You wonder how they miss you to be honest,
throwing their stuff over the walls.
But they do miss you

most of the time.
One of my mates, he got hit, though,
I say hit,
by a shower of Afghan fingers.

Suicide bomber in the road outside.

Normally the alarm gets you first
but even then you'll be

wow,

wow,

something is real.

My friends at home
can't understand what I'm saying.
It's the anticipation I'm used to.
It's the news I'm waiting to hear.
No rumours,
everyone quiet and waiting for the facts.

Surreal, if I'm honest.
Surreal when I get back.

The ease. The slow pace.

In Subway, for instance.
Cucumbers. Tomatoes.
You think:
Get it done *now*, so everyone can go!
Just come on!

Then you leave
and road works are everywhere

with nothing moving,
and rain pattering down,
and clouds covering the stars.

The war debts will come out then.
You think:
my weapon.
where is my weapon?
And you look for it.
You did everything with your weapon
and it's like
urgh.
You miss it.
Nobody understands.
You miss it.
You went to the toilet with it.
And the shower with it.
You went running with it.

You did everything with it.
If you had a doss bag,
you kept it close as you could,
or in your doss bag,
sort of thing.

It's trust, you see,
you have to trust your weapon.
It's individual.

I'm Stephen North.
Lance Bombardier Stephen North.

2.

FICKLETY

This time we were looking at transition, the next incarnation.
It's interesting. Soldiers carry a lot on their hats, you know,
and we talk together about sadness, the ficklety of mortality.

One man, he was always getting sand out of his nose and ears,
and as more sand came to him, more and more sand and dust,
he counted it; he knew how many grains of sand there were.

As for me, I read the Psalms. The Wilderness. The helplessness.
The rocks, stones, wind and thorn trees. I encountered them all.
But a dog collar? No. Collar crosses instead and a tactical flash.

Then I came home and here are my children and my little list:
roof needs fixing, grass needs a cut, the long green grass,
we need such and such for the kitchen, bathroom, everywhere,

and aaah I've wrapped the car round a tree, aaah. It's interesting.
Now I think we are beginning to see the bow-wave of trauma.
Therefore I go with the men sometimes, pray for them always.

3.

Life So Far

My mother was keen to celebrate birthdays—
still is.
When I turned 25
I got her cake on exercise in Brecon,
my friend Tom
pulled it from his rucksack for me—
he'd been carting it round for a week.

Then I got cake again
in the Mess before we went to head off.

Afghanistan is something I wanted,
really wanted;
I've always enjoyed being outside,
playing in the woods.

First job
was Ground Holding in Central Helmand,
a base the size of a tennis court,
15 people,
actually good
for someone who doesn't have a house so far
or anything.

We patrolled a lot on foot,
maybe 8 or 10 hours each day;

if you think of the country
like a map of the Underground
we were pretty safe in Zones 1 and 2.
Further off in Zone 4
it was more kinetic,

which I'd say refers to enemy action
when they're shooting at you,
a good insurgent presence.

After that
we went to the desert country west of Sangin.
1000 metres above sea level,
absolutely bare and cold.
At night I dug this hole
only a little larger than my body;
I was very cosy in my down jacket,
with a warm sleeping bag,
and a thick mat.

I was making a nest,
with everything tucked in.
It's a strange one.
All night I was just a pair of eyes
with the sky running over me,
not sleeping,
looking at the stars and the black horizon,
not seeing any depth.
There's something to be said

for thinking earth has been here a long time.
Everything feels sweeter
coming back to camp after that.

Trees for instance.
and poppy fields in April and May—
field after field of poppies—
then desert,
then more blocks of colour,
pink and red and white.
and compounds showing up green,

and clear blue skies
above brown walls and barbed wire.

Really quite good actually.
You've made your decision,
you want to lead men in an operation.
But you don't want to die,
not much,
so you're always looking for ground signs,
a patch of disturbed earth,
a wire poking out
or an antenna,
and you're always totally unpredictable
about where you are,

erratic,

finding the most difficult way
to get anywhere,
avoiding bottlenecks and crossroads,
cutting through hedges,
constantly observing,
in and out of the ditches which were—.

Well,
you're carrying 50 kilos of equipment,
wearing body armour plates front and rear,
smaller ones on both sides,
knee-pads, gloves, glasses, helmet, chin-strap,
ear-piece for the radio,
thick Lycra shorts to protect against the blast,
also a heavy thing like a nappy.

Amazing how the body gets used to it.

You sweat and sweat
and you don't hold anything back,
you just sweat and accept.

Once a week
we went down to Helmand River,
cliffs one side
and the other a wide green zone,
and no we didn't swim,
the current was too fast.

But we did stand there in our full armour,
and we saw the country opening
right the way up to the mountains.

Another time
it was 4 o'clock in the morning,
June,
and we needed to cross a ditch,
actually more like a river,
a narrow river and straight,
with trees either side
and the moon shining between them.

I stepped forward.

I stepped forward into the water
and I felt my feet
lose touch with the bottom,
and I was just
'O goodness, I'm sinking',
and my legs were floating away
but it was all fine
to get wet,
it was fine,
and go through onto the high ground again.

4.

The Programme

I'm an army brat. I was brought up
to love the army. Basically I now do
army intelligence work. I'm aged 20.

It was difficult for Mum to start with.
Take good care of yourself she said;
keep your head down; be a grey man.

But you can't do that, no. You see it.
You see it and you think it isn't real,
until you get smells and other things.

I miss the gym, did I mention the gym?
I did the Insanity Training Programme
and I loved it. I followed that through.

5.
TALKING TO THE MOON

22 years   I've been in the army
my husband   we were   at Sandhurst
together
and 5 years after

courting I think is the word

I'd done Bosnia by then
in a tented camp   with the floods
and guys ringing home   with water
up to their knees

so with his tours in Ireland
Iraq
Afghanistan now
I do understand   I do
I've been there
I've done that

but hey
I don't want to hear

the day
he sent me a bluey
I took it   I looked at the map

mistake   a giant mistake
I thought   don't need it
I don't

we have 4 children   and Freddy
14   he's quick
much quicker

stop   stop   stop   stop   stop

I set up the choir   I've started my art

Sharon and Franny and Pam

I don't know   what I would do
injured
or broken   you just think
crikey

also there's writing
but actually I am so   hey
but at least you're twisting the lid

or you look at the mountains
they take you away

who could be there
who has explored them   who
is living there now

also the sky

if the children
are wanting to talk
I say to them   talk
to the moon   Daddy does that
you can talk to the moon together

then there's the bunting

it's hardly   like Christmas
but listen
it comes with us everywhere
we have a box

embarrassing really   never mind that
no one will see it this time

this time when he's home
we're tucked away in the woods.

6.

CRITICAL CARE

Jesus! Stay still! Stay fucking still!

Stay with us! Put morphine on it!

Don't touch it! Don't touch it!

We've got to get him out now!

We've got to get him out now!

|||||||||||||

All the way across on the slide.
Everyone ready?
Slide

|||||||||||||

You're back in England now.

My name's Clare
and you've got three of us you lucky boy.
Kate and Hazel and Clare.

Now just take a little break
in your breathing again.

Good lad, good lad,
you're doing very well.

But it's not the best day you've ever had, is it Andrew?

||||||||||||

The explosion has driven
a whole load of sand
and mud and rubbish
up into the tissue planes,

and of course the bugs,
they've got in there,
and they love it.

They've got a lovely warm moist wound,
lots of nutrients,
and they think they're on holiday.

||||||||||||

This is Mum,
Mum's come to see you.

and Natalie was on the phone
asking how you're doing.

She's waiting for me to tell her
everything's all right.

But it's not, is it babes?

Well,
we'll wait for the morning
and see how that goes.

||||||||||||

We're going to try and save the other leg,
his foot still has a pulse.

We're going to use topical negative pressure,
suction if you like, or a vacuum.

The bugs really don't like it.

||||||||||||

If you knew what there was in store for you
you wouldn't have your children.

||||||||||||

The blast also ripped the gums from his teeth.
This thing here,
this is a bit of grass from an Afghan field.

||||||||||||

Natalie's with me now.

she says the baby's
kicking the crap out of her,
don't you love?

||||||||||||

The surface of his eyes are so badly burned
a special membrane has been imported from America
to help reduce scarring.

It's the best chance he has
of regaining some sight.

||||||||||||

Now is really a waiting game.

All you do is wait.

||||||||||||

Unfortunately
the foot doesn't look very good.

Dusky.

The decision to operate depends on several factors.

||||||||||||

I told you I'd be back to hold your hand
didn't I, love?
Here I am. I hope you can feel me holding.

||||||||||||

Sister could you get a power amputation saw?

An amputation saw on power?

||||||||||||

I imagine his first thoughts will be
it's better off dying.

||||||||||||

As long as you can sleep peacefully
after making the decision
then you have made the right decision.

And I think we will sleep peacefully
after making the decision today.

||||||||||||

We find on the whole
when we do take the station off,
and allow them to wake up,
they are absolutely terrified.

Then we keep having to stress
they are safe now.
They are safe now.

||||||||||||

It's all looking good.

It's all looking very good in fact.

What we do next is take a sliver of skin,
a graze,
like when you fall off your bike.

Can I give you a bit of skin?

||||||||||||

You are sort of coming round now,
aren't you love?

You've been here three weeks
and you've been injured.

Yes lovey you have.

You've been here three weeks
and I've been at your side.

You've been injured.

||||||||||||

He's been nodding yes and no
and squeezing my hand.

I can't tell
what the no's are about.

||||||||||||

You still remember what's wrong don't you?

No?

You want to hear again?

You've lost your legs.

Yes two of them, both of them.

Please don't push me away, mate.
Please don't push me away.

||||||||||||

Andrew lives every day.

He lives every day for a hopefully.

7.
One Tourniquet

It was a long time ago
but I was there,
a combat medical technician.

I saw
children and IEDs
which wasn't nice at all.

One boy:
he had shorts and a dirty vest,
he stood on a mine;
he was conscious at first,
screaming,

and I thought
what a mess.

All in a bit of field.

None of the other kids cried,
they're all sort of tough.

Very tough kids in fact.

Definitely.

At the time
we were issued with only one tourniquet each.

But Camp Phoenix was down the road
and he went there.

A double amputee.
We heard later he survived.

So yeah. Brilliant.

Everything is hard.
Everything they've got to do
everywhere they've got to go.
Just hard.

I used to imagine
little towns in the country
nobody knew.

Little towns nobody had touched.

There would be people living there
all the same.

Just living there
in the vastness.

8.

THE GARDENER

In Memory of Lieutenant Mark Evison

We spent
many hours kneeling together in the garden
  so many hours
    Mark
liked lending a hand

watching *Gardeners' World*

building compost heaps

or the brick path with the cherry tree
that grows over it now the white cherry
  where I thought I mustn't cry
I must behave
  as if he's coming back

‖‖‖‖‖‖‖‖‖

It was just after Easter
with everything in leaf

  he is so sweet really
    but worldly
      before his time

I kissed him and said
                    See you
in six months   and he turned

    he turned and said

||||||||||||

I opened the garden for the first time

the National Garden Scheme

    you know
          what gardens are like in May

and this man was hovering around
          outside the front

as we walked down the side passage
    he said
          I'm a Major

I said   Oh my son   he's in the army
    sort of brightly

||||||||||||

Then I was alone

so I went
        and I gardened all day

how slow   how satisfying

I felt next morning
        he was struggling for his life

||||||||||||

He would be home
    with three transfers
        on three different planes

and if he died they would ring me
        and they would go back
            and they would not keep coming

my daughter Elizabeth and I drove to Birmingham
my mobile   there   on the dashboard

we had worked out the times of the last plane
and we arrived
    and they still hadn't called me
        and he was still

||||||||||||

He was lying   he was
with this
      Mark
with this big plastic hole
      sort of
a bandage over a hole
      just like
asleep

ıııııııııı

the reindeer   the wild reindeer
      giving birth in the snow
            with the rest of the herd scarpering

they have seen the eagle above them

but the mother stands still

      what am I going to do what

a bit restless   and everything
      but starting to lick her baby
with the eagle   watching

ıııııııııı

Quietened   that is the best word
to describe it   I felt quietened
seeing the hills below
      as we came into Kabul

I was thinking

            Mark lived in a very green place
and here everything is purple
      orange   Turner colours I call them

In my nightmares he is never dead
bandaged   lost   never dead
with my love
            circling
      nowhere to go

I was thinking

            thousands of lives
                  in an instant
and the molecules starting again
      and the mountains never changing

how was I
      quietened
            how

but for a moment
    I was
then losing height
    with the brown earth rushing to meet me.

THE FENCE

I found my way home but it was not until summer
ended that my mother brought herself to ask me
to make good the fence that marks our boundary.
I went out there with a box of nails and a hammer
and when a flock of crows in the trees surrounding
made some comment, I remembered how the birds
living by Shamash Gate spoke in perfect harmony
with mortar shells falling. Then I began knocking
nails into the wood and everything near took fright—
although not my mother, who continued watching
from her chair on the porch. I have said nothing yet
of what it is like to reach the exact point where one
place becomes another, with no way forward or back,
and there is nothing else left to do except fall down.

III.

POEMS

(2009–2015)

FIVE PLACES FOR KYEONG-SOO

1.

Kwangju

When I come to the border around midnight
holding your amazingly light body in my arms,
your feet kick suddenly and we cross over.

There is your grandmother walking ahead of us
along a narrow ridge between the paddy fields,
and kiss-kiss is the sound of her black sandals
making peace with the earth then taking leave of it.

2.

Montauk

Remembering how a wave made in Antarctica
preserves its shape for many thousands of miles
provided the water is fathomless and only starts

dying when the ocean bed shelves towards a beach
whereupon the crest still travelling unhindered
gradually topples forward ahead of the toiling feet

with no choice except to disperse the energy it kept
so long in store, we caught the train out to Montauk
and were content all day to walk the windswept shore.

3.

ORKNEY

We stopped for no particular reason I could see
beyond the bridge across a burn that hurtled
off the tops and into Harries Loch. But doubling
back into the twilight of the arch where grass

had made a secret lip to catch the water's breath,
we found the otter's feasting stone beside the track
that ran between one disappearance and the next.

4.

HOME FARM

The hare we disturbed in the yard of Home Farm,
that either limped ahead of us or bounded or both,

paused whenever we at our dawdling pace dropped
out of view, and so seemed to be leading us onward

past the deserted cattle pen and twilit barn
stacked to the rafters with blue barrels of poison,

until we came to the wide gateway and the grazing
where it turned for one last look, leaving us a view

of tall grass shining in the wind which was beautiful
enough but now hid something we thought we knew.

5.

HOLY ISLAND

I am behind you on the mainland, leaning
on your shoulder and pointing with one arm
in front of your face at weightless cinders
which are ravens drifting above the island.

Boulder clay on the outcrops, and beaches
dotted and dashed with coal dust. Guillemots
whitening the cliff face. Small orchids apparently
still evolving in a downpour of Arctic sunlight.

How many years are there left to cross over
and show you things themselves, not my idea
of things? 25, if I live to the age of my father.
I cannot explain why I have left it as late as this.

Your black hair blows into my eyes, and I see
everything moving fast now. Weather polishes
the silver fields ahead. The ravens swoop down
and settle in the gorgeous pages of the gospels.

WHALE MUSIC

1.

In the beginning I found it very difficult to believe
I was in fact alive. Was I a creature or a country?
I decided creature, and at the same moment also

discovered my voice. It was not so much a form
of communication with others as a way of proving
I was alone in the world, which has remained true.

Nevertheless, I continue to announce my presence,
speaking in tongues that create a definite shape
for everything I see, which is a glassy universe

without borders, crossing-points or territories,
let alone walls or doors, light or dark. Only currents,
fluctuations of temperature that mean almost nothing,

and sometimes, if I surface, the moon- or sun-light
in which I cannot fail to notice that by living slowly
I have become a catastrophic danger to myself.

2.

When we abandoned our lives as gods or curiosities
we neglected to develop a sufficient appetite for safety.
The times you dashed at us with boats and harpoons

we might have dived down out of range but instead
stayed in clear sight and died. You could say therefore
the impression of wisdom given by my colossal forehead

is a complete illusion—except as we gathered together
making only confused and feeble attempts to flee
we proved something you are still failing to understand.

3.

I can confidently say I was never more amazed by my own size
than the day Brendan the Navigator and his flock of monks
managed a landing on my back in the midst of their isolation.

Presuming me to be an island, they then lit a fire of driftwood
and said Mass in thanks for their Salvation. In their sleep later
I ferried them to shallow water, where in time they went ashore.

4.

When first recorded by listening devices my voice
was understood to be the ocean floor creaking
which is a means of calling it the loudest sound

of any creature that has passed through the world.
Other impressions I give are very gentle clicks;
a squeak like an immense underwater prison door;

clangs like the same door slammed hard shut
every seven seconds; and Morse code suggesting
human talk. This is the most recognisable sound

to you, and also the most mysterious since it allows
a perfectly good idea of what it is you want from me,
although how you might reply you know less well.

5.

Now she is long-gone I can only speculate
and make that my existence. I heard her speak
once, a pressure through water like a wave

inside a wave, but I never set my eyes upon her.
The green chambers of my interminable palace
were deserted—emptiness succeeding emptiness.

It was the same when I dived down to the depths.
Was she there? Not so far as even I could make out.
The life I have without her is apparently complete

and doomed, but I deny this has made me a failure.
Like her, I am a prisoner of the splendour and travail
of the earth, but grateful to prove I have existed at all.

6.

I have given you many long and tall stories to complete;
millions of soft lights; an excellent means of lubrication
for watches and other fine instruments; delicate bones

for corsets and strong ones for decoration and building;
the good edible meat of my body; and not to be forgotten
ambergris—which one scientist has said reminded him

of 'An English wood in Spring, and the scent when you tear
back the moss and discover the cool dark soil underneath'.
My last gift of all will be the silence of your own creation.

AN ECHIDNA FOR CHRIS WALLACE CRABBE

Whatever kind of determination a creature needs
to enjoy one state of existence before confronting the next
the echidna has a-plenty.

Look how the legs which once upon a time were fins,

then paddles,

and now are covered with spines as delicate as fur,

shunt this specimen up the barren mound
that forms the one significant feature of his pen,
still hampered by the excessive weight of his body
but clearly not enough
to feel distracted from his main ambition.

Which is to reach this particular point
by the concrete wall that marks the limit of his freedom,
where he shovels the earth aside with his rubber snout
before giving up when roughly half-submerged.

He has no idea
anyone is waiting for him at the end of history.

But he obviously understands
that to start again at the beginning
and change faster
would only mean taking the straight road to extinction.

THE DISCOVERIES OF GEOGRAPHY

If only the stories were not so tempting—
but from day one I started to embroider,
and in no time was suggesting a country
far to the North,
where fish are as large as dragons,
and even minor administrators
eat off gold plates
and sleep on gold beds.

This is why I have packed in my birch canoe
a robe
made of the feathers
of more than 100 different species of bird.

So that when I have finally crossed the Ocean
I will have a ceremonial costume
rich enough
to impress in my encounter with the Great Khan.

⁞⁞⁞⁞⁞⁞⁞⁞⁞⁞⁞

We have an excellent long boat with outriggers
and therefore travel dozens of miles in a day.

Furthermore, and speaking as a navigator,
I can predict every fickleness of weather
and also the change in direction of currents,
sometimes dipping my elbow into the water

and sometimes my scrotum
to feel the slightest change in temperature.

These are the reasons
I shall be considered a saviour by my people
and die in peace.

In my own mind I am a simple man
who threw his spear at the stars
and landed there himself.

|||||||||||||

I now have in my possession a map:
two handfuls of mud
scraped from the bank of our sacred river,
flattened into a tablet,
baked,
then pierced with the blunt point of my compass
while I spun the other, sharper leg
to produce the edge of the world as I knew it,

and beyond,
the salt sea on which I am perfectly at home.

In this way I look down at myself.

I think: I am here.

|||||||||||||

Astonishing how many horizons are open to me:

at one time mountainous heaps of smashed slate,

at others a vast delta of green and crimson light.

And every day a different shore-line ripples past
bearing its cargo of white sand and dark palms.

Very beguiling they appear, but all encumbered.
All spoiled by the tantrums of their local gods.

Out here there are storms too,
but in the religion I have now devised for myself
I am convinced
the shaping hands have pulled away from us at last,
so the earth hangs with no support at the centre of—
what?
That is the question I have in mind to answer.

IIIIIIIIIIII

You might suppose better charts would help me,
but in spite of their much greater accuracy
in terms of coastlines and interiors,

and the intricate detail
guaranteed by developments in printing,

not to mention the understanding of perspective,

empires still lie about their extent and stability.

These are the simple deceptions.

More difficult,
as I continue North to my final encounter,
and wave-crests flicking my face grow colder,
and daylight a more persistently dull dove-grey,
is how to manage my desire to live in the present
for all eternity,
as though I had never left my home.

iiiiiiiiiii

It transpires the last part of my journey
requires me to abandon everything I once knew,
even the gorgeous costume
made of the feathers of more than 100 different species of bird.

No matter, though.
It is delicious among the constellations,
as the planets begin to display their gas-clouds
and the beautiful nebulae their first attempts at stars.

When I look over my shoulder
to see my own blue eye staring back at me,
I realise before I disappear
I still accept what it means to be lost.

THE CONCLUSION OF JOSEPH TURRILL

Garsington, Oxfordshire, 1867

I suppose I was cut out for a quiet life;
whether I have managed any such thing
is another matter,
what with larks to shoot,
and harvesting, gooseberries, and whatnot.

Then there was all that with Netty:
would she or wouldn't she;
did I or didn't I?
It is my belief
I spent more hours kicking my heels at her gate
than happy the other side.

But heigh-ho.
Anno Domini drives out stern matters of fact,
and faults that appear to us
when we compare the lives we have
with those we imagine. . . .
There's nothing a gentle stroll
in the woods by moonlight can't put right.

I tried that just now.
I saw swallows on the branches like clothes pegs,
which put me in such good humour
I brought home one of their nests and also four chicks.

THE DEATH OF FRANCESCO BORROMINI

for Peter Maxwell Davies

1.

The architect Borromini, born Francesco Castello
in Bissone on the shore of Lake Lugano in 1599,
is dying in Rome as dusk falls on 2 August 1667
by his own hand. The point of his sword has narrowly
missed his heart, which by good luck or bad judgement
means he has time to summon a priest and confess,
also to recall what he must leave behind in the world.
To the confessor he freely admits it was impatience
at not having a candle to continue working in the dark
that persuaded him to point the sword against his chest
and fall upon it. Meanwhile in S. Carlino, his earliest
and still-unfinished masterpiece, the last sunlight burns
down through the eye of the dome like an angel arriving
to ask of those within: *Which of you has been my servant?*

2.

In the hollow earth beneath S. Giovanni dei Fiorentini
a crypt as immaculate as a blown egg is the setting
for the most intimate and intense theatre of his death
and life. Someone, an already grief-stricken friend,
has left a pair of women's ballet shoes by the altar,
setting them neatly side by side and then departing.
The suggestion is that whoever it was understands
the weight of stone is the same as the weight of air
and, like a breeze blowing across a field of wheat,
will sway, curve, vault, bow, spin, stop and stand
with a visible force and leave the clear impression
of things by nature continually unseen and invisible,
or like a dancer, their white shoes printing the stage,
pounding it, even, but only to leap upwards and vanish.

3.

S. Giovanni in Laterano is the next place of pilgrimage
for his dying mind on its final inspection of everywhere
that proves the thing it was. Medieval brick cries out
beneath the new, austerely swaggering stone: *Mother
and head of all churches in the city and upon earth.*
Echoes crumple into the bays; they rise and multiply
under the glamorous roof; they glide over the tombs
where death is already ensconced and grinning. Each one
is pitch perfect. It is like watching a parliament of crows
at sunset, when the whole sky darkens with their arrival
and, above and beyond their big racket of conversation,
creaking wing feathers take complete control of the air
as many thousands of birds swoop into their own places,
where in a second they fall silent and will suddenly sleep.

4.

While there is still light the eyes will operate, organising
now the flight of the mind into the Oratorio dei Filippini,
and the first example of a small but exceptional innovation—
namely, a balustrade on the upper floor based on triangles
formed by three concave arcs, set with the bulge appearing
alternately at the top, then the bottom. A quite novel shape.
The eyes rejoice in it, discovering here too is a kind of dance
and also a vantage point, an actual way through the marble
(white marble, streaked with grey-green, and coarse-grained
with shining crystals) to other examples of his close attention:
the cupboard in the refectory, for instance, with divisions
in which the Fathers kept their napkins; or the *lavamano*
in the vestibule, that takes the form of a large black tulip
with four petals standing, four spread out to hold the water.

5.

Now it is the turn of the tongue, wondering how to speak
at last of S. Ivo alla Sapienza, the old university church,
where six bays represent the body, head, and four wings
of the bee, which symbolises the Barberini family, but also
the star of David, since the significance of stone continually
shifts its ground without moving. By much the same means
the confusion of Babel tongues blathering all over the tower
might also be a sign of wisdom, the gift of tongues, in fact;
or the very form of the vault—an immense marquee of light—
could be persuaded to reappear in a small tent-like silk cover
placed daintily over the tabernacle containing the sacrament.
There, the tongue wants to say and the brain too: *the meaning
of this is definitely that.* Then the incandescent brass bell tolls:
Never one thing. Never one thing. Never one thing. Never one.

6.

In a glimpse of the afterlife, Borromini now claps his eyes
on the leading twentieth-century interpreter of his work,
the university professor, Surveyor of the Queen's Pictures,
Director of the Courtauld Institute and Communist spy
Anthony Blunt, climbing back stairs with special permission
to reach the roof of the Palazzo Falconieri. Here he finds
something not easily seen at street level: a concave loggia
crowned by a balustrade carrying Janus herms, whose two
faces in each case make a striking silhouette against the sky.
One looks over the tangle and rumpus of the city; the other
across the Tiber to Trastevere. As soon as the difference
is clear, all eyes that can turn now look in the same direction,
to see the long river carry away everything it still reflects
over the raking weirs and beneath a succession of bridges.

7.

The last light is still sliding in a single weak column
through the dome of S. Carlino where he observed it
in the beginning, inscribed with fine curlicues of dust.
Borromini lies down and places his right eye exactly
under the beam, so it becomes a telescope to heaven—
except he is looking through the wrong end, and sees
only his young self setting out, complete with a plan
that matches his delirious heart to his meticulous brain.
There is no mistaking the brilliance of this, or the damage
he will do to himself. Jealousy and hypochondria. Rage.
Genius and more rage. Then the light disappears entirely.
With the sword run through my body I began to scream,
and so they pulled the sword out of my side and put me
here on my bed; and this is how I came to be wounded.

A LATE PORTRAIT OF AUDREY WILLS

I was a Brixham girl
and Dad's boat was
    the pride of the fleet

every day
    when they came ashore
        I had my pick of the mackerel
beautiful
    shiny blue suits

then again
    I was stationed on the flying boats
that was a lovely time
they came in   very low over the water
    or seemed to

ask yourself
    what will you remember

in Llandudno   on honeymoon
singing at night   can you hear me
singing   and
I painted my toenails red
    I still do this
        by myself
that's me there
dancing round and round the house
without a single brown penny in my purse

you see what I am saying
    I am living
every colour except grey

    and   you would not believe
    I have
looked after everyone   yes
but I have
    when I go to the doctor now
        I find the   door closed
          do I knock   what
do I do

I sing

come in   I am Richard   I landed
on Gold Beach   I am Peter
        I was married to Steve for 57 years
        I am Helen aged 72
     and I do tatting
    I am Ali a widow   I am Ron
and I enjoy boiled potatoes
    and a drop of broth
      I am not a lover of sweet things.

as for me   I am Audrey Audrey
    open the window
        and let me hear the seagulls
          let me hear the seagulls flying across

as for me   I love God and   I want to die
    what better thing is there   to live for

THE REALMS OF GOLD

In a quiet part of Leamington Spa,
in the same flat
where he has lived all his life,
sixty-two-year-old Michael Standage
is close to completing his biography
of the poet D. J. Enright.

Nobody reads Enright now
apart from a few surviving friends,
and a handful of fans
who insist he is under-rated.

Standage does not speak to them.

He is nervous of an interpretation
that differs from his own,
and they are jealous of him;
it's not as though his book
is authorised or anything;
he just got there first
and found that archive in Japan.

All the same Standage
is confident of a clear run home.
He works late each night,
and only pauses
to watch a black wind stirring the trees
that line his side street but stop
where it meets the main road.

Meanwhile the poems of D. J. Enright
gather dust in second hand bookshops
or fly into a skip
along with other unwanted things
that go when a life ends.

A long history of adventure and homecoming.

A fastidious editor yet free
to travel in the realms of gold.

A highly original mind
with Proust among others
virtually off by heart.

And speaking of the heart . . .

But to date only Standage can do that
with any confidence.

The rest of us, the few
of us,
open the dark green *Collected* and think:
this was a life as good as any;
who am I to let it vanish completely
without returning an echo?
When I read him and I listen
to the silence following,
I know
exactly what he means.

Standage makes an exception to his rule
and accepts my invitation to meet.

We decide on Brighton,

which is neutral ground,
and walk for an hour on the shingle.

Following publication
can we look forward
to a revival of Enright's fortunes?

We both sincerely hope so,
and while the dry grey stones
grind under our shoes,
extol the virtues for which we feel
a common admiration,
especially as they appear
in *Paradise Illustrated*
and *The Terrible Shears*.

Once we have reached our climax
we stand still
and stare out to sea.

Small waves beat towards us,
fold over neatly, and turn into foam.

Very soon more follow and
the same thing happens.

THE FISH IN AUSTRALIA

Where the mountains crumbled
and yellow desert began,
when the sun began to smoulder
in a vault of indigo,
I left the metalled road
and found a perfect circle
of still and silent water
fifty yards across,
with hard treeless banks
un-marked by any prints.

Call it a pool of tears
wept by dogs and kangaroos
or dead transported men.
I considered it a dew pond,
but no dew anywhere
ever fell that swarthy colour,
or seemed so like the lid
of a tunnel piercing through
the planet's fiery heart
to the other side and England.

Providence anyhow
had made me think ahead,
and without a moment's pause
I had parked up on the bank,
had my rod and spinner ready,
and was flicking out a cast
to see what rose to me.

Nothing rose, of course.
A kookaburra guffawed
a mile off in the bush
and a million years ago;
a snack of tiny flies
sizzled round my lips;
and as the dying sun
sank deeper in its vault
a gang of eucalypts
in tattered party dresses
seemed to shuffle closer
and show their interest
in hearing how my line
whispered on the water
(now uniformly solid
ancient beaten bronze),
how the reel's neat click
made the spinner plonk down,
how the ratchet whirred
as I reeled in slow enough
to conjure up the monster
that surely slept below.

As I reeled in slow enough
then suddenly too slow,
and the whirling hooks caught hold
of something obstinate.
Not flesh or fish-mouth though.
Too much dead weight for that.
A stone age log perhaps.
A mass at any rate
that would not change its mind

and snapped the flimsy line
which blew back in my face
as light as human hair.

If not myself at least
the pond lay peaceful then,
with sun now turned to dust
and a moon-ghost in its place
as much like company
as anything complete.

Why not, I thought,
why not,
despite the loss to me
continue standing here
and still cast out my line,
my frail and useless lash,
with no better reason now
than to watch the thing lie down
then lift and lie again,
until such time arrives
as the dark that swallowed up
the sky has swallowed me.

SWIM

We quarrelled over something
     I don't remember
and   while you slept
I tried to make good
     by mending a broken pipe
     under the bathroom sink.

When I hit my head on the rim
I decided   to hell with it
          I'll spend the afternoon
taking a swim
          instead.

And why not
     prove myself
          capable after all
by ploughing across the harbour
          and back?

Given that meant   a mile
and all manner of shipping
     including a liner
     recently in from Barcelona
I had to strip off   and go
before I finished the question.

Breast-stroke
     crawl
          breast-stroke

then for a while
floating
    getting my breath back
until the liner
    set sail for Barcelona again
which kept me treading water
    as long as the huge beast
        swung from the dockside
            out
    surprisingly quick   and yet
slow
    sloshing an oily ripple
        over my head as a joke
before
    looming above me
        capped with faces shouting
Look out!
    or
        Look!

I was still treading water
    treading
        water   but thinking
it will be time soon
        to kick myself forward again
what with the liner
    sliding away from me now
    juggling the world in its wake
this way and that   then
    shouldering off
        through the harbour mouth.

Achille Lauro.
that was the name I saw.
    Achille Lauro.

    Wasn't it
captured by hijackers once
    didn't they
shoot   what was his name
        Klinghoffer
then tip him overboard
    out of his wheelchair?

I could return to that   I would
    later return to that   but now
I was half-way across only
half-way across the harbour
    legs suddenly stringy
breath
        short
    and still   still a good way
    from starting the journey back.

What had I   ever   been thinking?
    What had I
        not been thinking?

You   I thought
        you will never need know
not if you
    never wake up.

It could be still
     an afternoon like the others
the lazy others we spend
     here on the island
in Caprichosa   in Cala Rata.

I might   really
     I might not remember
          how the enormous water
opened beneath me

how
     a liner
     had easily slipped straight over
and through

how I swam onwards a little
     rested
then swam onwards again
     until it was all
behind me
     all the silvery harbour
catching the light of late afternoon
     and I was back here in our bedroom again
          still lying beside you.

OF ALL THE BIRDS

1.

MAGPIE

The magpie I like least
who stole my wedding ring
thinking it was his

to hide it in his nest
along with glass and pins
and other shining things.

2.

NIGHTINGALE

In the pine wood which grows on the sand at Es Grau
rumour has it there are nightingales. Clematis we did find,

thick yellow and gold like honey turned back into flowers,
along with sea-holly and white lilies in the perpetual shade.

3.
PEEWIT

It was all down to my kite needing
space not available in our valley
and finally I decided on a field

already planted with winter wheat,
even though the ground was rain-sodden
and the farmer would crucify me if he saw.

A peewit kept me company, broken-
winged and weeping, *Over here!*
It was almost enough to tempt me

to some act of violence, but never mind
as long as her plan saved the nest
with its clutch of speckled eggs.

4.

DIPPER

One you showed me nested
on the far side of a waterfall,
another in what became a bubble
trapped when the water rose.

In all events the dipper marks
his passage with a flinty note
scraped against the softer sound
of everything that water says.

Then ups and quits his rock
to walk along the river's bed,
as if a living soul had found
a way to haunt the dead.

5.

CORMORANT

When it came to leaving
I went with the cormorant
flying well below the radar
and breasting the muddy lake.

Down the road was his double
at home on a rotting fence-post;
shabby wings hung out to dry
closed in the breeze of my passing.

THE MILL

Over the road
and twice the size of the house we lived in
    five stories at least
        white clapboard
            wide as a barn.

The cat reconnoitred.

I followed the cat
    clambering
        this side or that
of the mounting-block steps
    then ducking the sack
    that drooped like a sleepy eye
    almost to block the door

and in.

Darkness.
        Light.

Shadows that
      jigged with bran-dust
      and wheat-dust
and softened the pulleys
    the beams
      the ladder fading away
      towards this attic or that
    where the miller must be

ignoring me
on my porridgy floor.

And hushed.

But roaring in fact
    the dry
    continual
    biblical
    thunder
    of mill-wheels
    grinding together.

Surely
the heaviest weight in the world.

Furious too
with a fury of infinite patience.

        Where was I now?
I'd forgotten.
        No no I remembered.
        Looking for something
    I was
like the cat looking
        here between rows
        and rows of comfortable sacks
        like soldiers asleep.

Looking for this
    perhaps
        this handful of grain in a gush

overflowing my hands
at a rickety tunnel
like money but free
and precious   priceless

if only I caught it.

Maybe not this.

Maybe just wanting
the doorway again
what with the weight at my back

the weight
and darkness
breathing and grinding.

Look.

Was that really my home there
over the road?

That acacia tree by the gate.

That border of pinks.

My mother's face in a window pane
like a bubble
frozen in water.

Surely again
    surely
        surely not mine.

Besides
    I had turned into dust.
White hands
    white clothes
        white hair.
And next thing would float away
    through white air.

LAYING THE FIRE

I am downstairs early
looking for something to do

when I find my father on his knees
at the fireplace in the sitting-room
sweeping ash
from around and beneath the grate
with the soft brown hand-brush
he keeps especially for this.

Has he been here all night
waiting to catch me out?
So far as I can tell
I have done nothing wrong.

I think so again
when he calls my name
without turning round;

he must have seen me
with the eyes in the back of his head.

'What's the matter old boy?
Couldn't sleep?'

His voice is kinder than I expect,
as though he knows
we have in common a sadness
I do not feel yet.

I skate towards him in my grey socks
over the polished boards of the sitting-room,

negotiating the rugs
with their patterns of almost-dragons.

He still does not turn round.

He is concentrating now
on arranging a stack of kindling
on crumpled newspaper in the fire basket,

pressing small lumps of coal
carefully between the sticks
as though he is decorating a cake.

Then he spurts a match,
and chucks it on any old how,

before spreading a fresh sheet of newspaper
over the whole mouth of the fireplace
to make the flames take hold.

Why this fresh sheet
does not also catch alight
I cannot think.

The flames are very close.

I can see them
and hear them raging
through yesterday's cartoon of President Kennedy

and President Khrushchev
racing towards each other in their motorcars
both shouting
I'm sure he's going to stop first!

But there's no need to worry.
Everything
is just as my father wants it to be,
and in due time,
when the fire is burning nicely,
he whisks the newspaper clear,

folds it under his arm,

and picks up the dustpan
with the debris of the night before.

Has he just spoken to me again?
I do not think so. I
do not know.
I was thinking how neat he is.
I was asking myself:
will I be like this? How will I manage?

After that he chooses a log
from the wicker wood-basket
to balance on the coals,
and admires his handiwork.

When the time comes to follow him,
glide, glide over the polished floor,
he leads the way to the dustbins.

A breath of ash
pours continuously over his shoulder
from the pan he carries before him
like a man bearing a gift
in a picture of a man bearing a gift.

THROUGH THE LYCH GATE

All Saints, Stisted, August 1900

Thousands of heavily-seeded grass-heads
    are waving through the lych gate
I have entered countless times
    to find the churchyard always very trim.

This must be
    because the mower and his scythe
        cannot be spared at harvest time
    besides which
the dead are not many.

Charles Morgan Forster is here
    and the crafty builder who designed
        the twisted chimneys in the main street
seems to be a recent arrival.

But the dozens of crosses and head-stones
    packed on the slope
        down to the river
do not exist yet

and the empty ground by the flint wall
   where my great-grandfather
      and my great-grandmother
         my grandfather
         my mother
     and my father
lie in their descending order

is just that,

empty ground,

where I have yet to stand and imagine
   the bliss
      of having never been born.

Acknowledgements

The poems in 'In the Stacks' were commissioned by Poet in the City and the London Archives, and were written in response to items held by the British Library.

'Peace Talks' was broadcast in a slightly different form on BBC Radio 4 on 11 November 2014, under the title 'Coming Home'. All the poems in this series are based on interviews I held with British soldiers and their relatives in Spring 2014, mostly in Camp Bad Fallingbostel in Germany. I am very grateful to the following: Lance Bombardier Stephen North ('War Debts'); Padre David Anderson and Sharon Anderson ('Ficklety'); Adjutant Michael Altenhoven ('Life So Far'); Lance Corporal Ben Johnson ('The Programme'); Major Wendy Faux ('Talking to the Moon'); Ranger Andrew Allen, Linda Allen, Chris Allen, Major Clare Dutton, Lt. Col. Steve Geoffrey, Senior Care Nurse Erica Perkins, and everyone associated with the 2009 BBC TV programme 'Wounded' ('Critical Care'); Sergeant Vicky Clarke ('One Tourniquet'); Dr Margaret Evison ('The Gardener'). I am also grateful to the producer of 'Coming Home', Melissa Fitzgerald.

Several of the other poems in 'Laurels and Donkeys' are best described as 'found poems'—which is to say they contain various kinds of collaboration. Some use the words of others without much alteration, others edit and re-arrange an existing text, and others combine existing sources with my own words.

The title and most of the content of 'An Equal Voice' are taken from the historian Ben Shephard's book *A War of Nerves: Soldiers and Psychiatrists, 1914–1944* (Pimlico, 2002). To this degree the matter of the poem is in the public domain. The poem is also indebted to *Shell-shock* by Anthony Babington (1997). Further acknowledgements are as follows: 'A Moment of Reflection' to *Black Lamb, Grey Falcon* by Rebecca West (1941); 'Setting the Scene' to a letter written by Captain Ted Wilson, quoted in *Weeds* by Richard Mabey (2010); 'Laurels and Donkeys' to *The Old Century* by Siegfried Sassoon (1938); 'The Life of Harry Patch' to *The Last Fighting*

Tommy by Harry Patch and Richard Van Emden; 'Beyond All Calculation' to *Medicine and Victory* by Mark Harrison (2004); 'John Buxton' to *The Redstart* by John Buxton (1950); 'Changi' to *Within Changi's Walls* by George L. Peet (2011); 'The Station at Vitebsk' to the Memoirs of Bella Chagall, quoted in *Chagall: Love and Exile* by Jackie Wullschlager (2008); 'Coming in to Land' to *The Unreturning Spring* by James Farrar (1968); 'The Minister' to 'A Visit to Iraq' by Gordon Campbell (unpublished); 'Losses' to *The Good Soldiers* by David Finkell (2009); 'Op. Billy' to Robert Mead, Ministry of Defence Press Officer, and Captain Dave Rigg MC, the Royal Engineers, quoted in *Spoken from the Front*, edited by Andy McNab (2009); 'Vallon Men' to 'The Marines of 40 Commando are Back from the Front' by Karen McVeigh, the *Guardian*, 18 November 2010; 'The Fence' to *Yellow Birds* by Kevin Powers (2012).

I acknowledge the following sources: *Borromini* by Anthony Blunt (1979) for 'The Death of Francesco Borromini'; *Leviathan* by Philip Hoare (2008) for 'Whale Music'; *A History of the World in Twelve Maps* (2013) by Jerry Brotton for 'The Discoveries of Geography'; *An Oxfordshire Market Gardener* ed. Eve Dawson and Shirley Royal (1993) for 'The Conclusion of Joseph Turrill.'

Andrew Motion was poet laureate in the United Kingdom from 1999 to 2009, and is the 2015 winner of the Ted Hughes Award for New Work in Poetry for his collection *Peace Talks*. The author of several biographies, he won the Whitbread Prize for Biography for his authorized life of Philip Larkin (1993). He has published a memoir, *In the Blood* (2006), and two acclaimed young adult novels based on Robert Louis Stevenson's *Treasure Island: Silver* and *The New World*. Cofounder of The Poetry Archive, Motion was knighted for services to poetry in 2009. He is currently Homewood Professor in the Arts at Johns Hopkins University, and lives in Baltimore, Maryland.